Weather Wise

Clouds

Helen Cox Cannons

Raintree is an imprint of Capstone Global Library Limited, a company incorporated in England and Wales having its registered office at 7 Pilgrim Street, London, EC4V 6LB – Registered company number: 6695582

www.raintreepublishers.co.uk
myorders@raintreepublishers.co.uk

Text © Capstone Global Library Limited 2015
First published in hardback in 2014
The moral rights of the proprietor have been asserted.

Edited by Siân Smith and John-Paul Wilkins
Designed by Philippa Jenkins
Picture research by Ruth Blair
Production by Victoria Fitzgerald
Originated by Capstone Global Library Ltd
Printed and bound in China

ISBN 978 1 4062 8477 5
18 17 16 15 14
10 9 8 7 6 5 4 3 2 1

British Library Cataloguing in Publication Data
A full catalogue record for this book is available from the British Library.

Acknowledgements
We would like to thank the following for permission to reproduce photographs: Dreamstime: Azathoth973, 13 (bottom right), Eaglexr, 21, Jakerbreaker, 14, Mvildosola, 12, Nantheera, 16; iStockphoto: Imageegaml, 11, JLBarranco, 18, scol22, 13 (bottom left); Shutterstock: Alexey Repka, 15, C_Eng-Wong Photography, 13 (top left), elen_studio, 13 (top right), Gwoeii, 5, irin-k, 22, Jacek Chabraszewski , 19, jeka84, 9, konzeptm, 8, Maria Meester, 10, patpitchaya, 20, Samuel Borges Photography, cover, Zacarias Pereira da Mata, 17

We would like to thank John Horel for his invaluable help in the preparation of this book.

Every effort has been made to contact copyright holders of material reproduced in this book. Any omissions will be rectified in subsequent printings if notice is given to the publisher.

What are clouds?

water droplet

Clouds are made of many tiny drops of water. Each tiny drop is called a **droplet**.

Contents

These droplets are so tiny that they float on air.

How do clouds form?

When the Sun warms water, some of the water becomes a gas called **vapour**.

The vapour rises into the air. Then it cools down and turns into droplets. These droplets make clouds.

Types of clouds

Clouds can be many different shapes.

Some clouds are white and fluffy.
You may see these on a sunny day.

Some clouds are grey. You may
see these on a rainy day.

10

Some clouds are very dark and thick.
You may see these on a stormy day.

Some clouds cover the sky. You may see these on a snowy day.

12

cirrus

stratus

cumulus

cumulonimbus

Different clouds have different names.

Cloud colours

Clouds look white because of light from the Sun.

Sometimes clouds can look dark
and grey. This is because they are
very thick.

How do clouds move?

Clouds are moved by the wind.

Wind pushes some high clouds
very fast. They can move faster than
a car on a motorway!

What do you wear in cloudy weather?

Cloudy weather means it might rain. You may need a waterproof coat or an umbrella.

18

Sometimes cloudy weather can still be warm. You may not need a coat at all.

How do clouds help us?

Sometimes water droplets join together in clouds. They fall as **raindrops**.

Living things need water to stay alive and grow.

Cloud quiz

What clouds might look like this?

Answer: Cumulus clouds might look like this.

Picture glossary

 **droplet** tiny drop of water

 **raindrop** group of droplets

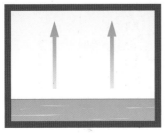 **vapour** gas made by heating water

23

Index

Notes for parents and teachers

Before reading
Assess background knowledge. Ask: What is a cloud? How do clouds form? How do clouds help us?

After reading
Recall and reflection: Ask children if their ideas about clouds at the beginning were correct. What else do they wonder about?

Sentence knowledge: Ask children to look at page 7. How many sentences are on this page? How can they tell?

Word recognition: Ask children to point at the word *water* on page 6. Can they also find it on page 21?